COLLECTED POEMS

Aarushi Raj

DAGUERRE PRESS

Collected Poems by Aarushi Raj
ISBN 13: 978-1-950888-09-2
ISBN 10: 1-950888-09-6

Copyright© 2023 by Aarushi Raj

All rights reserved.

No part of this publication may be reproduced, distributed, or transmitted in any form or by any means, including photocopying, recording, or other electronic or mechanical methods, without the prior written permission of the publisher, except as permitted by U.S. copyright law. For permission requests, contact the publisher.

DAGUERRE PRESS

COLLECTED POEMS – Aarushi Raj

Contents

Introduction 1

The Eternal Summer 3

In About a Billion Years 5

The Raging Storm 6

Rejoice 10

The Mythology of the Universe 11

Defiance 13

By the Candlelight 15

A Stranger's Land 16

Does the World Cease to Exist? 17

Fear the Flame 19

Cold, Cold Reprobate 21

Dreary Dreams 22

The Dull World 24

It Almost Led Me to My Grave 25

Open the Door 26

The Land of Rainbow 27

Revenge 29

The Pain of Parting 30

The Magic of This Day 31

Nothing Good 32

Sunlight and Moonlight 33

Mist and Sunshine 35

A Voice Calls 36

Colors Unknown 38

The Thoughts of an Unfairly Accused Criminal 39

A Flame Flickers Inside 40

Rain 41

Ice 42

The Two Halves of My Soul 44

The Shadow of Sunlight 45

Introduction

Over the span of more than a decade, from my early childhood through my transformative adolescent and teen years, I have penned my evolving understanding of the world and my thoughts and emotions. **Collected Poems** is a window into this journey. Through these 30 poems, I would like to share with readers the thoughts and emotions of my formative years.

Drawing from the wellspring of nature, the contradictions of life, and the intricate tapestry of emotions, each verse paints the multifaceted spectrum of existence. These serve as a reflection of a young mind navigating its way through the meanders of youth. Just as a summer day may bestow both brilliant sunshine and stifling heat, our lives are an amalgamation of joy and sorrow, where discerning one from the other becomes an intricate dance.

For me, poetry is a haven where words spring from deep inner contemplation. Through this anthology, I invite readers on a voyage through wonder, amazement, fear, love, loss, hope, despair, courage and all the nuanced emotions in between. By sharing them, I want to emphasize the universality of our emotions, regardless of the paths we traverse.

Aarushi Raj
August 7, 2023

1.

The Eternal Summer

What I see is but a cheerful and pleasant scene.
It is the season of summer when grass is most green.
The flowers are more beautiful than ever before.
But to this loveliness, could there be more
Than what at first sight might appear?
Could misery exist in the brightest season of the year?
But questions are not needed, as now it is so plain
That unclouded these skies must remain.
Once they could disguise the keenest pain.
And bring solace with the sorrowing rain.
Before, this unhappiness was not my own.
But now this truth is clearly known.
Often the desolate wind had blown.
And brought with it mournful cries.
But unclouded are now those skies.
All of the sorrow is now mine.
So brightly that the sun does shine
So that the truth is so clear.

Broken must be the bonds that were so dear

In order to feel ever any relief.

Still, I cannot rid myself of this grief.

But my fate may not be as it now seems.

Perhaps my hopes can bloom as they did in the past.

The eternal summer cannot forever last.

But I cannot always be so blind

For this agony will always weigh upon my mind.

2.

In About a Billion Years

In about a billion years,

Something will happen greater than all our fears.

For those who don't want this, it will be an unpleasant surprise.

In a long time from now, the sun will become a red giant and

So large in size

That it will burn up planet Earth,

The place of our birth.

How can we prevent

This terrible event?

I wish this idea could be proved wrong.

But on Earth, we might not last long.

3.

The Raging Storm

Let the rain fall more
Furiously than ever before.
Let the winds blow and blow
As they have never blown.
Let the rain overflow
And inflict more misery and pain
Than ever before.
Let no desire or triumph remain.
Let all that was kind, honorable, and true
Face this miserable rain and fade.
Let there remain neither shelter nor shade.
Let the miserable and hopeful clash.
Let truth be defeated in a conflict that was more rash
Than ever before.
Let this illusionary world disappear
And fade away into the unknown.
Let everyone experience the renewal of every fear
And dreams they have never dreamt before.
Let this rainfall last longer.

Let this storm rage on and rain
More than ever before.
With it, let suffering be felt by everyone.
The force of the flood will be stronger
Than ever experienced before.
Let this storm last.
Let this despair be unrivaled by the past.
Let this glorious sun
Never rise upon a world I never knew.

My hopes have flown away with this falling rain.
My attempts to restore them have gone in vain.
From this wind and rain, my heart has been chilled.
Those dreams and desires of before have been killed.
Am I to lose everything I have only to lose more?
This existence is impossible to restore.
Yet are these dreams buried so deep?
Will Hope awake from her eternal sleep?
Eternal this sleep always seems.
Darkness seems to have destroyed my dreams.
Yet if it only seems, what is real?
What do my presentiments wish to reveal?

It is a parting cloud, I am sure,
Signs of the end of a storm more chilling than ever before.

Let the rain cease and no longer pour.
Let this misery and desolation fade away.
Let this raging storm turn into obscure mist.
Let this rainfall leave no sign
As to suggest it ever did exist.
Let dawn signal the arrival of a brighter day.
Let this beautiful sun shine
More brightly than ever before.
Let pleasure and joy take pride
In a triumph more glorious than ever before.
Let those who suffered no longer hide
From a world they began to fear.
Let all sorrow disappear.
Let the wind never blow
As harshly as it once blew.
Let all those plants who were weakened grow.
Let the flowers bloom more
Profusely than ever before.
Let this world be reborn.

Let it no longer mourn

A distant, fading past.

Let this happiness last

Longer than ever before.

An existence it will restore,

In which pleasure and relief will be felt by everyone.

Let this bright and glorious sun

Never cease to rise upon the world I never knew.

4.

Rejoice

What once was cause to rejoice
Now troubles my mind.
It seems strange that my hope, once so strong,
Could fade and that my dreams could fall
To enemies unknown almost overnight.
For a revival, I have no right to long.
Once, I had the greatest strength of all.
Even in the darkness, there was forever light.
My hopes blossomed like dawn.
But now I no longer have the choice
To change my future and alter my fate.
I can only rejoice in that pain that once was gone.
As I once knew happiness, I rejoice.
Because there was much before to anticipate,
Because I once knew how to be blind,
I will forever rejoice.

5.

The Mythology of the Universe

Beginnings

The story of how the universe became what it is today

states that at the beginning, the world was orderly and calm.

From that single thought

that existed to never change, the King

was born, and he sought to make world stay

its simple, orderly way,

for there was great peace which his aim brought.

Change

There cannot always be peace;

tranquility will always have to cease.

The King's world soon became less serene

as an angry thought formed into the Prophetess,

who thought the way the world operated was wrong.

However, she possessed beauty the king had never seen

and could predict the future, which was beyond the abilities of his.

The King soon became fond of her and asked her to be his queen.

She gave him no answer and said, "I may say yes if you would expand

the universe with me, for I know that is how the world will surely

be, as in the future, I can see."

And she smiled, and her eyes twinkled,

displaying their sparkling shade of grey.

The King agreed, and a new world he and the Queen began to create.

They ruled with a powerful bond.

The Present

Times changed before long.

Before long, there was an entire world that existed.

Before long, the cosmos was an extraordinarily disorganized and yet systematic place.

Before long, the mind of a mortal would seek to unite all the scattered wisdom of the world.

6.

Defiance

Wondered, wandered, and pondered have I,
Thinking this world I sought to defy.
Yet I still could not deny.
That this world was not mine.

I have looked out for every promising sign,
Thinking this world was one I could defy.
I have struggled with failure, unhappiness, and stress.
Still, I have learned from such struggle and have experienced
The dear delight of sweet success.
I have wondered how I could exist
To disappear and vanish
In the obscurity of mist.
Such thoughts of defiance I cannot banish.
They will dominate and control my mind.
For from only them, solace I can find.
I wish not to blend; I wish to shine
As bright as the brightest light

That exists in the sky.
Common truths I must deny.
This world I must defy
If I wish for it ever to be mine.

7.

By the Candlelight

By the candlelight,

Much comes into sight.

By the candlelight, much is dared.

By the candlelight, less is spared.

Reality is a mere shadow.

More longing and pain come with these dreams.

But by the candlelight, there is no darkness in the night.

Stronger feelings cannot be felt

After the candle will completely melt.

Yet for a long time, its ray of hope gleams

For those who seek comfort with its warming glow.

8.

A Stranger's Land

How familiar, yet alien this land seems.

I seem to still be haunted by memories of being an outcast.

Peace I can still find in broken dreams.

Their influence will forever last.

The waves crash upon this desolate shore.

A rushing calm comes with each wave.

They save me from the tranquility I abhor.

They save me from the despair this shore once gave.

And the shore leads to a stranger's land.

It seems as bleak as I foresaw.

A place whose ways I still cannot understand.

And these ways are the law.

9.

Does the World Cease to Exist?

Does the world cease to exist,
Or do I?
Both I find to be true as time passes by
And as my understanding is reduced to obscure mist.

Never has there been a darker day.
Never did my world become so faded and unclear.
Everyone so ardently dear
Has left me alone.
I knew, like others, that the world was not my own.
But why was I the one I chose to betray?
I have lost my identity and sense of pride.
My hopes have all died.
For recognition, I always strive.
Only with it, I can thrive,
Or else I will wither away.

How dreary the world seems!
For the pride and success, I live for

Are no longer mine.
I live as a person I abhor.
Yet if this hope is not mine,
Is this despair and pain?
I am still another who is of hope as sure a sign
As the first ray of the rising sun.
An inspiring individual who is free
From the mistakes of the past.
Who can and will sustain
Me through every difficulty and is more
Determined and thoughtful than I could ever be.

10.

Fear the Flame

Fear the flame; do fear the flame.
Touch it once, and your life will never be the same.
Do not be fooled by its impressive glow.
This is the same deadly fire that caused
All Earth's creatures to perish.
Rivers of fire underneath Earth's
Surface still flow.
Fear the flame; do fear the flame.
Meddle with it once, and you
Will be the one who deserves the blame.
The world you love and the people you cherish
May turn to mere ash
If you will be rash.
The eye of destruction's feared glare
Is not to be witnessed, so beware.
Fear the flame; do fear the flame.
This deadly fire is difficult to tame.
It wishes not to obey,
For it has its own way.

This deadly fire set the Earth ablaze.
Not a soul did remain.
Yet the sun tried to comfort with its faithful gaze.
The world was full of loss and pain.
Do fear the flame; touch it once,
Your life will never be the same.

11.

Cold, Cold Reprobate

Cold, cold reprobate. Why do you come
Once more?
Why do you return to a world you
Abhor?
Your soul has been blown
By the wind to the land of unknown.
Your body is in your grave.
From your miserable fate,
No one can save
You, cold, cold reprobate.
Unearthly vision, the very sight of you
Makes me shiver
And makes my lips quiver.
Return to eternal peace, for though your
Existence was quite brief,
It caused great misery and grief.

12.

Dreary Dreams

Such lovely dreams I long to dream.
Yet with them, drearier the world will seem.
Welcoming will always be their sight.
Yet they will always weep and moan.
A very painful loss they will never cease to mourn.
After such dreams, morning is never bright
But is filled with thoughts of a love unknown,
Of ambitions and hopes yet unborn,
And of desires to become only such a dream.

Such frightful dreams I know I must dream.
Yet without them, the light of my hopes will never gleam.
They are as beautiful as dawn's every shade,
As enigmatic and mysterious as the sea,
And as dismal as the darkest night.
But they must always begin to fade,
And become nearly unknown to me.
Brief is the moment when they provide light.
I fear to become such a dream.

Aarushi Raj

All this while, I wonder while I dream.
Without dreams, darker the world will always seem.
I know they bring back echoes of the past.
They are as lovely as short-lived spring
But are also as faithful as the season.
The influence they have will always last.
Comfort and hope they will always bring.
They give my life a purpose and a reason.
I can only long to be such a dream.

13.

The Dull World

I looked with increasing alarm
For the world had lost all its charm.
The world is beginning to fade.
It is becoming an ugly gray shade.
Oh! How much duller
Is the world without its bright color!

14.

It Almost Led Me to My Grave

My love for you has never ended.
Unfortunately, affection for me and desire
To ruin my life in you are blended.
How can you be cruel and cold-hearted?
How different are you from the last time we parted?
I heard you wanted me dead,
So why am I still living?
Why am I always the one
Who has to be forgiving?
My hopes of happiness are shattered.
To you, has it even mattered
What would I feel?
My wound will never heal.
The deep affection I gave
You returned, but you still caused me
Unhappiness that almost led me to my
Grave.

15.

Open the Door

Open the door.
I know this is what I am meant for.
I can't wait anymore.
I know before I have tried
To escape it and have cried.
But now leave my side.
I have seen that the path that is mine
Is not full of sunshine.
I know leaving this room
Might lead me to my doom,
But let me out of my jail.
I do not care if I fail.
I cannot stay here any longer.
But I will be stronger
When I am weaker
And of shades, no longer remain a seeker.
I do not dread
What is ahead.
You have opened the door at last,
So I can do what I dreaded in the past.

16.

The Land of Rainbow

There is a land of Rainbow
Where I often go,
A place only a few people know.

Sometimes I'm in a hurry
To escape my world of worry.

Sometimes I enjoy the route
With its beauty before my eyes.

I then go to a place
That many people say is full of lies.

Many people do not understand
How evil exists in this land.

If from your home, you go too far,
You will forget where you are.
Challenges you will start to fear,
And you will not want to go home from here.

The land of Rainbow is
A land where people don't notice the time
The sun decides to set,
And a land where
People see the sun
Rise with regret.

Even better, it's a land
You can control and where you can find
That what is false is true.

17.

Revenge

Revenge is a hideous monster which can
Turn kind people into people others dread.
On a large scale, Revenge can cause
Many people to be dead.
For in all times,
Revenge has made
Innocent people commit crimes.
Revenge pretends to be your friend
When it actually is your foe.
And Revenge creeps up on you when you're low.
Seeing Revenge isn't rare,
So beware!
You should fear Revenge
And run away when it is near!

18.

The Pain of Parting

I cannot bear to hear the sound of
The closing of a door.
The door closes on all the bright
And cheerful prospect of before.
Much sorrow and unhappiness comes
From that dreadful sound.
To relieve this unhappiness,
No source of solace can be found.
Much influence and power has that
Sound that I dread to hear.
This simple sound is one I always fear.
It is a sorrow difficult to explain.
Powerful bonds it can destroy.
From such separation, there is never joy.
From parting, there is only pain.

19.

The Magic of This Day

I held on to the magic of this day,
Hoping for it to never go away.
I know these simple pleasures
Will be nothing less than treasures.
I looked resentfully at none;
I smiled at everyone.
It was so perfect, and I decided not to cry.
Instead, I looked at the beauty of the Earth and sky.
Oh, how delightful is the Earth to me!
It has so much beauty to see.
I looked at the moon,
Knowing that night would come soon.
Then the sun, big and bright,
Would announce the end of the night.
I looked in front; I looked behind.
I am trying to fix the beautiful picture in my mind.
I delight in the gentle emotions I feel.
I cannot believe this day is real.

20.

Nothing Good

There is nothing good left; that's clear.
This place is inhabited by sadness and fear.

Even night isn't night,
And even light isn't light.

Misery and gloom
Are in every room.

One time, cheerfulness was there.
And unpleasant feelings were rare.

But the happiness died,
And to get it back, no one tried.

Oh, what unhappiness there is every day!
It is confusing that in this place, people choose to stay.

21.

Sunlight and Moonlight

Sunlight is beautiful and bright.
And quiet and calming is moonlight.

Sunlight boasts of its beauty all day,
And moonlight comes in a modest way.

At its zenith, sunlight boasts
Too much, harming people's skin.

Moonlight shines lightly and
In your house, it doesn't even get in.

Moonlight is calm and sweet,
But sunlight gives you more than a treat.

It is the reason we can live on Earth,
The reason for life's birth.

Moonlight is so calm and can soothe anyone,

But I prefer the boastful yet life-giving light from the sun.

22.

Mist and Sunshine

I am the mist over the sea.
Obscurity defines me.
I used to be bright sunlight
Known to everyone in sight.
I treated people unfairly on one side.
Now, to reconcile with them, my hopes have died.
On the other side, the way I was treated was unfair.
Now I am of nowhere.
I have no place to belong.
Thinking how my actions were wrong,
I have forgotten no one
But am remembered by no one.
I am, in short, of no worth
Or consequence to anyone on Earth.

23.

A Voice Calls

The wind is furiously blowing.
On a boat, I am rowing.
"Come, back," a voice calls.
But between us, there are many walls.
I don't know where this path may lead,
But I will not come back regardless of how
Desperate is the plea.
There are no clouds in the sky.
The weather is very hot and dry.
"Come, back," a voice calls.
But between us, there are many walls.
I don't know where this path may lead,
But I will not come back regardless of how
Desperate is the plea.
Snow gently falls on the land and river.
It is frozen, and I begin to shiver.
It grows warmer, but blocking the way, there are many fallen trees.
I am stung many times by angry bumblebees.
I am not blind, but I cannot see.

Aarushi Raj

The journey never scares me.

My decisions are hasty, yet they are the best I can make.

My answers to people are true,

Yet within them, there are always ghosts of lies.

24.

Colors Unknown

The color of many things will remain a mystery

To you if you think colors aren't given to things you cannot see.

Have you ever thought that there is color in music's sound?

Music is a gorgeous rainbow, and if anyone saw it,

The smile they had been searching for would be found

What is the color of the dreams we hope to come true?

It is a deep beautiful shade of blue.

What is the color of math, which some people like

And others wish they didn't have to know?

It is a lovely violet from the rainbow.

What is the color of victory which causes much pride?

It is pretty golden who with itself is quite satisfied.

25.

The Thoughts of an Unfairly Accused Criminal

I would have thought
That someone like me would be so distraught.
Dreadful stories try to give me fright,
But in darkness, I see light.
I did not, of course, relent.
I know that I am innocent.
It is the duty of the people of the future
To decide that my accusers were unjust.

26.

A Flame Flickers Inside

After I face sorrow and pain,

I realize that myself I need to restrain.

I wish to be cold, calculated, and wise;

The world I will despise!

Yet a flame flickers inside, and it refuses to be blinded by pride.

Is this a loving, true, honest soul?

No, it is a passionate wretch I must control.

My heart is and always will be concealing

True and tender feeling.

It will never take me by surprise

That a flame still does flicker inside.

27.

Rain

Rain
Saves our
Fields on fire,
Burning with rage,
Delays our grim graves,
Reminds us to seek life
That is still beyond man-made.
The droplet's dance will forever last.
When the world began, it was simple.
It seeks a similarly quiet end.

28.

Ice

Between my reality and dreams
Ice has frozen and become a river.
Frigid and fearful the world seems.
It is so cold that I begin to shiver.
This river is a mirror of my fate.
And my days will not be bright.
I do not have anything to anticipate.
And not even the brightest sunlight
Can ever suffice to thaw this ice.

I live in a world of my own imagining
With quaint villages with lovely streams
And gardens with flowers of every hue.
And the majestic castles reach the sky.
But this world is also chilled by ice.
And its destruction I always fear
For it always begins to disappear
When I even begin to think of it twice.
I cannot remain despite how much I try.
To this world, I cannot remain true.

Nothing hopeful comes from dreams.
Solace or certainty they cannot bring.
My life seems very useless, unhappy, and bleak.
Yet I think hope will someday return.
To fulfill my dreams, I will always seek.
And in my heart, a fire always burns.
And from this day, I always will strive
To keep alight this furious flame.
So one day, I will be able to thrive,
And my life will not always be the same.
My life has promise because of this fire,
For my dreams can become real.
And I can achieve what I desire.
And sorrow I will no longer feel
If my fire can ever suffice to thaw the ice.

29.

The Two Halves of My Soul

I am no longer whole;

The barrier of time separates the two halves of my soul.

I am now only the present half, a situation I loathe.

How complete I would be if I possessed both.

Myself I do not even recognize.

I recognize the color, shape, and size.

But I do not recognize a soul so black

And this reprobate.

Such a person I do scorn and hate.

I wish the other half I did not lack.

In the past, I see a person so different.

What happened after

Those days of laughter?

I don't know if I will ever find out.

30.

The Shadow of Sunlight

I can almost feel the scorching heat and smell the freshly cut grass.

A pleasant world I can see through a window glass.

Yet to enter this world, I am forbidden.

From sight, however, it is not hidden,

And I am greeted by only the shadow of sunlight.

I stand in a dark, dreary corridor, waiting for time to pass.

I bear a burden too heavy for one soul.

Myself is one I need to console.

A pleasant world lies before me, and to enter this

World, I never entreated anyone,

As I am only greeted by the shadow of sunlight.

A lovely, cheerful scene comes into sight.

It is a world so distinct and clear,

So far away it is, yet it is so near.

But I shall only be greeted

By the shadow of sunlight.

***

www.ingramcontent.com/pod-product-compliance
Lightning Source LLC
Chambersburg PA
CBHW030140100526
44592CB00011B/978